# The Indigenous Peoples of the Earth Book of Prayer's

Invocations
Anisazi People of America
by Wisdom Keeper

Copyright 2015/ Copyclaim RaDine America. – Author

F.I.A.A.H.~ Institute for Indigenous America Studies.
School of Ancient Wisdom &Healing Arts
All rights reserved

No part of this book may be reproduced or transmitted in any form or by any means, graphic, electronic, or mechanical, including photocopying, recording, taping, or by any information storage retrieval system, without the permission, in writing, from the publisher.
Produced by; Quantum Leap SLC Publications
admin@fiaah.org  www. FIAAH.org

ISBN: 0-978-0-9705455-4-1      Printed in America

# Dedication

Indigenous Peoples of the Earth book of Prayer's is dedicated to the Anisazi people of the Americas aka Negro peoples and all indigenous children of the Earth, who look like the soil, who are the SOUL of the planet Earth. May these words of wisdom keep us strong to withstand the power of Destruction against us and all of our planet Earth....

Especially to my son Marcus-Lazar B., Joemarik, Morgan, Brittney, Liberty, Zaire, Kristin, Andrew.
A special thanks to Sister Stephanie Butler and Elder Brenda Murray.

# Acknowledgements

This Sacred text was derived from the Life prinsciouness of Earth, I want to thank the Life awareness's of Earth for choosing me to share these precious words with our people. These prayers are invocations from the heart of life itself. With the power to bring corrective focus and changes needed to save ones life...

RaDine Amerca- Wisdom Keeper

The Indigenous Peoples of the Earth Book of Prayers is one in a series of books as part of Americas Heritage Outreach Ministry.

The Institute for Indigenous America Studies ~ School of Ancient Wisdom & Healing Arts.~ Indigenous Ministry Program's is for Indigenous people of America who have the calling to service for healing the wounds to the emotions of the original Earth created people of America, by using Indigenous methods from the Anisazi cultural traditions of Life heritage with the Americas. To learn more or enroll

www.indigenousamericastudies.institute

Other Books by Quantum Leap Publications SLC
Author; RaDine A- America
The black America's Handbook for the Survival for the 21st Century series;
Intro-The Hidden Ancestral Identity of the American Negro
Vol. 1. The Forgotten Truth behind Racism in America /final Edition
Vol. 2. Books for Life
    The Book of Life
    The Book of Principles
    The Book of Earth Heritage

# Contents

| | |
|---|---:|
| **Intro** | 5 |
| **Why is Life important?** | 7 |
| **Basic principles about the nature of Life** | 8 |
| **The Earth Covenant for Life** | 19 |
| **Life Principles** | 27 |
| **Affirmations** | 37 |
| **Prayers** | 53 |
| **Meditations** | 69 |
| **Conclusion** | 95 |

# Introduction

For thousands of years indigenous people living with Earth used sound and thought to work with the emotions of our planet Earth. At one time all peoples living with Earth were created by Earth and understood their connection with the Earth as their great Mother/ Creator and their physical mother as the portals used by the Life/Nature of Earth to renew its cycle of physical experience as Life. Death as the release from the physical awareness of life in creation ,returning back to the essence of life force, awaiting the time again to recycle into a new physical experience .. The physical mother is bound in physical experience the primary mother is the Earth itself.

Our physical experience in Life of Earth is only as good as long we don't forget Life with Earth is bigger than the personal physical experience . All physical characteristics are expressions from life of Earth expressing itself and challenging us to change correct our mistakes, and grow..

For millions of years Indigenous people of the Earth, who look like the soil of the Earth, understood they are part of the Soul of Earth, kept themselves close to the Life Covenant of Earth or Soul , so they would never become ungrounded and stuck in the limitations of physical life. Living the lower destructive aspects that bring Death to Earth Life. Instead, they kept themselves connected to the higher collective planetary life flow with their physical life journey cycles and continued to grow with Earth as a part of Earth life awareness. This book helps an indigenous person strengthen their life force connection to the higher collective planetary life flow.

Keeping one's life experience flowing with the flow of planetary life is the purpose of affirmations, prayers and meditations. These tools help us intellectually navigate with the flow of emotion in life. Use the prayers and watch your life force grow stronger- – take corrective action and return towards the correct direction for your life journey to experience your greatness life purpose, and accomplish your Life destiny.......

Aqucheway,

Wisdom Keeper

The following pages are Sacred Text of essential Life principles, affirmations, prayers, and meditations to remember in thought to uplift and strengthen ones innate Life resolve for remembering  our true purpose for life we serve, in face of tremendous perceptions of adversity that we confront daily in our lives. Use the Life principles, affirmations, prayers, and meditations on a regular basis and you will strengthen the Life force within you and be able to stand strong to serve your life purpose and triumph against all odds.

Watch the grace of life fill and renew you,

Living in
Freedom Consciousness
is living without knowledge
about Earth and our
Life purpose.
Living without knowledge
of Life purpose is
enslavement-Freedom

Embrace LFE!!!!!
Let Life Liberation live again!!

# Why is Life important?

Life is the Emotion
of our planet Earth
(energy in flow)
governed by a
system of principles
which supports the
planet Earth's
viability or SOUL.
Without the process
of Life of Earth as
Nature there is no
Heaven or Hell, there is
no form of existence.
Nature is the collective emotion of Life
of Earth as the organic process for
keeping the planet Earth ALIVE.

## _Basic Principles about Life_

\*

Life is the emotional force of Earth flowing through YOU in your blood !!!!!

\*

All People find their personal expression by striving to fulfill their primary birth purpose for having Life with Earth. All people who strive to accomplish their highest purpose with Life receive the highest experience for Life. They live with joy, happiness, Health, Creativity, Peace, & without fear.

All people created by Earth are connected by blood of the Mother to a section of soil to Earth to be fruitful and multiply as their Garden of Eden.

People belonging to a Garden of Eden are called
"Indigenous " or SOUL People's

All people who look like the Earth(soil) are a very important part of the planet Earth organic internal Nature of the soil or soul of the planet Earth. We are another system within the planetary body of Earth
We are an extension of the life blood of the planet Earth.

We live through the life force of the planet Earth. We work for the Earth..

Indigenous people as Earth workers for the soil- represent the

keepers or stewards for the SOUL of Earth or soil environment as nature including animals they are connected to.

As stewards for the SOUL of Earth, as nature or environment. They are to Nurture, protect, and maintain the balance of integrated functions operating as Nature. Today this is called **<u>Natural Resources</u>**.

All collectives of Indigenous peoples belonging of the planet Earth have a combination of primary purposes to fulfill for the planet.

 Our birth placement from our mothers blood heritage of belonging to gender (M/F), race, ethnic population, and Earth soil section for the heritage blood represents where our life path is to fulfill our primary purpose needed for the continuation of Life with the planet. All challenges to Life can be solved thru following life principles to correct the mistakes of the past, trusting the fact.

"Essence of Life Awareness" is with you..

  Let go, Let Life take charge!

 ## Mistakes in Life Awareness

Indigenous people for the Earth have changed the primary purpose for their life with Earth into -A personal choice- when it is not.

Life is the Earths force or emotional awareness and our bodies are the physical means like a flying carpet or car used to navigate the physical ride thru Life's emotional growth journey.

Life itself is not a inorganic toy- its alive it is apart

of a larger organic process system of our planet Earth

    To love oneself means to respect and value the force of life with in you, and your collective inheritance as part of the "human" nature of Earth, recognizing you are a VALUABLE part of Nature, regardless of the corruptive (Parasitic/narcissistic, and selfish) ways for living with the life force is being experienced as personal/collective Life purpose today.

To Love means to nurture the growth/building of Earth Life

expression as Nature within each of US.

Those who Abandon the challenge to fulfill their primary Life purpose to Serve the nature of Earth, thru their GENDER function for life with Earth, receive little joy from their emotional in physical life journey and receive the experiences for the death of life has to offer- fear, weakness, loneliness, pain & suffering
Poverty

What is the primary purpose of a Female?

All females who look like the soil of the Earth represent the SOUL of Earth or emotional portals for Earth emotional force (Spirit) awareness expression for the continuation of NEW LIFE CREATION cycles, as SOUL Creators with Earth of their species. All females nurture the fertility in LIFE.

A females function is to continue the SOUL cycle of Life that all Earth created life forms depend on to flourish to live within Nature for her section of Earth as her Garden (soil). They serve this purpose by nurturing the Life of the soil or SOUL within the life force cycle of Earth their blood heritage belongs to.

A Female's primary purpose is to build Earths emotional awareness in physical forms, to create and nurture the growth of the SOIL by working with the elements that created them.

All people on the Earth are created by the life force within the female. The females create the populations of People living on the Earth. She is the generator of Life and holds the fertility of her kind.

The female has the power to create new forms of LIFE from emotion, and is responsible to develop the emotional awareness in the children, so the emotions within the people will always stay united and strong with the Life force awareness of Earth. (all emotions respond to an inner core directives called prisciousness).

# What is the primary purpose of a Male ?

 All Earth male's created by females for the Earth are the physical strength of Earth emotional force. The Earth males have the intellectual awareness for protection for the SOUL of Earth, and all living beings belonging in the garden(soil) he is connected to by his MOTHER'S Blood Heritage. Males function as all forms of protection including keeping the genetic quality of their species strong thru their pollination with the Earth females who created them, for continuing the growth of power for the Earth species with the Earth life cycle. All males protect the fertility for Life of their kind of people.

The Males develop the reinforcing/ building systems or structural support, which keep their inherited environment viability with Earth SOUL safe, strong, and resilient; implementing the collective emotions physical direction.

The male develops the physical aspects of intellectual awareness, so the intellect will know how to perceive and respond to the directives from emotional awareness or prisciouness

Females and Males combined efforts promotes

the continuation of the innate Earth Life SOUL force cognitive abilities to understand and correct mistakes with our lives that are corrupting and destroying our Earth SOUL, mistakes if not corrected, will result in destroying our ability to have positive life experiences. The process of cognitive (feminine and masculine) development into maturity creates UNITY, and sustains collective unity that allows us to have higher perceptional awareness of what is happening to Life of OUR PLANET Earth...

# The Life Covenant of Earth

All life created by Earth including human females of the Earth are ordained as a part of Nature with Earth . All Earth People (indigenous) are born to work with the Earth FREE OF ALL BONDAGE to MAN KIND - WITH A BIRTH INHERITANCE to live to serve their function purposes to their planet Earth freely FOR LIFE.

No Earth peoples or indigenous person are born a servant to another person, family, communities or alien races, No indigenous blooded person is born a human beast for burden.  (There is no need to stop or control the production of life of any Earth created race.)

All Earth created beings/species including, animals, plants, and human kinds have a unconditional place of belonging to SOUL (soil) somewhere with the planet Earth. This area of environment is where their "blood" birth-inheritance to natures Life support transferred to them thru the blood of the mother's only connection to the soil from the Mothers for the soil or soul with the planet Earth Life/Spirit. This placement is where they are to be fruitful and multiply,

All soil in their section with Earth belongs to the natural inhabitants by Blood OF THE MOTHER to the soil/Earth environment . All Earth sections belongs to the perpetual generations of the race collective/population connected to the soil.

All Earth/soil is to be shared among all living beings who naturally belong to it. People WHO NATURALLY BELONG TO A Earth /soil environment ARE CALLED INDIGENOUS or SOUL PEOPLE

All children represent the insurance or fruit for the race/ bloodlines to continue its healthy existence as a part of the harmony and balance that maintains the life-soil-eco-system of their soil placement with Earth as part of the SOUL of the Earth. This balance maintains the Earth's internal regenerative system for the planet Earth.

All knowledge from females of Earth about the eco life-soil--system connected to them, for how to continue the development of SOUL of Earth growth ,nurturing of life ,and

the comfort received from it, is called Heritage.

It is the duty of all people to respect, value and protect their birth inheritance from their mothers Earth heritage to soil, lifestyle, collective culture, and society from the intrusion of influence for exploitation from other foreign people, creatures ,hybrid forms of nature and non-organic as artificial things.

All females of all Earth-created races represent the portals for regenerative power for their race to maintain its cosmic/DNA existence or BLOODLINES with the soil as the SOUL Earth given for them to live with the planetary life- soil- eco- system. Only the people with the complete DNA for the Earth soil environment can be keepers for and regenerate their Section of Earth Life power developed for that eco soil system...

All females as well as all living planetary beings ( i.e. trees, animals, etc) have an unconditional covenant with the planet Earth to be fruitful and multiply ,for maintaining their DNA in the Eco system (Soil/soul) they was developed for, that will support all their natural needs with-in the planetary Earth system !!!!!!!.

Earth Life- soil- environments do not support Foreign/alien/ immigrants life blood needs in sections of Earth designated to a different bloodline of the SOUL for inheritance.(Example: America is the environmental ( forest) connected to the people who look like the Earth (soil) in America . Anisazi-aka Amerindians aka Negro females.

People who are not born from a Anisazi/ Negro female do not have birth inheritance DNA connection to soil of America. They do not draw complete nourishment from the plants with the soil.

Being Indigenous to Earth is not simply a membership...

It is an unconditional birth inheritance shared from the blood of our Mothers to have a place of belonging to serve our planet Earth, as an functioning part of the life FORCE system (Nature) with the planet Earth. It is something you value and protect for Life-with your life to keep the continuation of our collective life force cycle (Tree) of our soul alive with our planet called Earth.

AN EMBLEM OF AMERICA.

**Oh Great Spirit of Earth**
Whose voice I hear in the winds,
And whose breath gives life to all life of the planet Earth,

        HEAR ME!

I am small and weak, I need your strength and guidance.

Let me see the beauty, and make my eyes
behold the red and purple sunset that bring serenity to me.

Help my hands respect the things you have made and my ears sharp to hear your voice from the distractions.

Make me wise so that I may see what life has revealed to me and understand the lessons from the mistakes by our ancestors with Life in the past, and today that affect the future of myself , my people and Earth ..

Let me learn the wisdom you have to reveal in every leaf and rock..

I seek strength, not to be greater than my sister or brother, but to fight my greatest enemy—the Masters of the ego, that bring corruption of prisciouness leading to illness, disease and ultimately DEATH..

Make me always ready to follow your Prinsciouness,
with clean hands , piercing eyes, and open ears.

So when my Life cycle is done, the life force can return to the essence of Earth, and my being is content, and fulfilled with joy from my life journey……….
Aquecheway!

# Life Principles

## What does it mean to be Indigenous

To be Indigenous means:
My Life is the creation of the planet Earth.
To be indigenous means:
I am a child of the Soul force of Nature of Earth, in the image of Earth soil.
To be indigenous means:
I carry the original blood of The Earth in me.
To be indigenous means;
I am created to live in harmony with Earth and its creations, not mans..
To be indigenous means:
I am a part of Earth organic nature and have a unconditional place to belong with the planet Earth.
To be indigenous means
I have a life function as a part of nature with Earth.
To be indigenous means;
I have a purpose to serve in the life force of Earth.
To stand for your indigenousness means:
I have respect for my Life function & purpose from Earth
I value my home with Earth.
To claim your indigenousness means.
I help keep and build life for Earth.
To claim your indigenousness means;
I stand and protect the nature for life keeping Earth.
But most of all
To claim your indigenousness means.
I have a unconditional right to be free to live within my place of natural belonging with the Earth and to live to serve my life function & purposes for MY planet Earth.....
Aquechewa-Aquecheway-Aquchewa-Aquechewa

# Principles of A Indigenous Female

An indigenous female understands the power in her blood connection and the purpose she serves with her planet Earth. The blood of the planet Earth she carries gives her unconditional belonging inheritance to a section of Earth to thrive. This soil/soul is her collective garden, her place to be fruitful and multiply.

An indigenous minded female nurtures the development of her seeds as well as all seeds connected to her garden from Earth, for she knows her seeds are co-dependent on all seeds created by Earth to live with her in the garden. Without her union with Earth there is no garden-Life has no support for life. Earth life loses its inner support.

An indigenous minded female respects her life purpose as well as the purpose of others created to live in her life-support system.

An indigenous minded female knows she is very important to Life of Earth but not to the artificial world of mankind. She represents the Earth, when she fulfill her many functions in life of Earth she fulfills a function for the life support of her planet Earth.

An indigenous minded female is a creator, she creates beauty by working to uplift and give energy to all that she touches.

An indigenous minded female respects her life and the principles for life of Earth is how she is governed.

An indigenous minded female is not a selfish female living just for personal vanities or gain.

An indigenous minded female is a female who is aware of her power and the consequences from its miss use

An indigenous minded female is not swayed by the illusions or false comforts and fear of mankind.
But most of all an indigenous female allegiance is to her function and fulfilling her purpose to life for Earth and not to mankind. For she is the producer of all humanity and the mother of all indigenous males before they become men and deserves the highest regard, respect and value over all men...

## Principles of An Indigenous Male

An Earth centered or indigenous minded male understands his purposes and belonging to the planet Earth inherited from his Mother's blood is his shared collective garden. This is his place to have self determination and liberty. An indigenous male has the power from Life for PROTECTION of the lifes blood, providing security to keep harmony and balance for all he shares life with and respects all seeds connected to the garden for he knows his life is co-dependent on all he shares life with including the plants in the garden.

Without their Life there is no garden-he has no life.

A indigenous minded male respects his life purpose as well as the purpose of others.

A indigenous minded males knows he holds the key to the physical aspect for the emotional power of the Earth. He is to protect all Earth- created Life living with Earth, he is not the center of the world. He is the Protector for the Life of Earth and by fulfilling his purpose in keeping all life created by Earth safe he supports the cosmic whole of Earth..

A indigenous minded male uses his Earth power by building to keep security and harmony with all that he protects.

A indigenous minded male respects the life blood in his veins and the principles of life that empower him with the power from Earth to stop any form of destruction to his kind and his soil/ soul with Earth.....

An indigenous minded male is not a selfish person looking to capitalize on his Mother of life or blood of his people for his personal vanities or gain.

An indigenous minded male is a true male who is aware of his power and the consequences from its misuse.
An indigenous male living by indigenous principles will not be swayed by the illusions or personal comforts of mankind. But most of all an indigenous male's allegiance is to fulfilling his purpose for life of Earth and not to mankind For he is the protector and enforcer for the life force of Earth and of all humanity, and has the Ultimate physical power from all emotions with Earth. His deserves the highest value and respect.

## Let Gratitude be your Attitude

Everyday of your Life is a gift from Earth. Don't squander it. Don't waste it by being angry at Life because the events in your perceptions of life do not go your way.. Don't let it slip away feeling sorry for yourself.........

Be grateful for this precious gift of the blood of Life itself and remember your physical life is your personal gift from Earth, don't let the destructive vices of Man trick you to destroy it.

- "Let gratitude be your attitude." Appreciate your assets and talents, create with them to be a emotional expression for the glory of Life, don't let anyone rob you of being your true expression within you , purposely living everyday of your life striving to make a positive difference thru your life for life . Realizing that obstacles of man placed in Life are not the obstacles created by life, you will overcome and be triumphant in the end.

- When challenges flare and ego's dare, you settle back and remember a fact to stand strong is to stand humble and let Gratitude for life be your Attitude towards the gift of having the blood of life with Earth and watch how you will never have a sad day, for the power of your life blood will always shine on you every step of the way ~ Wisdom Keeper

## Principles of the Heart

 Principles of the Heart – Means it is our duty in every act, public and private, to follow our inner awareness of Earth principle ( prisciousness) without fear of want or rejection. Our aim, and purpose should be to fulfill your purpose to Earth well.

Below are ten ways to use our prisciousness as the basis for your actions, your allegiance to Earth will be accomplished.

1. Wholehearted acceptance that only the Life of Earth fills the universe of Earth.

2. The force of Earth is the source of all reality and is good.

3. Your goal in life is to be a expression for nature Life of Earth

4. You should rely on the spirit of Earth within you not on physical beings or material manmade things.

5. You get no ultimate gain or loss from material things, but only from the accomplishment you produce towards living for the expression of the emotion of Earth.

6. You should maintain focus of mind regardless of whether people praise you or blame you...

7. You should not make a show of spiritual activities to impress other people.

8. You should not be caught up in personal gain when you are working for life with Earths purpose.

9. You should hold life of Earth in reverence and be humble towards life.

10. You should use your inner Life awareness to understand your emotions and use the power from emotion with care and discrimination.

## Simple Principles for Life

### People who value the blood from their mothers as Earth, Earth will value them as its children.

**People who** live for the past live in the past.
**People who** ignore the mistakes of the past receive its consequences. People should recognize the contributions of the past but don't worship it.
**People who**   respect life will have a long Life.
**People who** live for the future will have a future.
**Anyone who** is not contributing to the upkeep, and viability for life is a parasite on Life.
**People who** chose not to support their own life are not entitled to receive support for life.
**People who** care for others who temporarily cannot support themselves, will receive help from others when they temporarily cannot support themselves.
**People who** no longer want to support their life. – you let go.
**People who** put learning and useing life- building skills first will always receive abundance in their life .
**People who** help others in building life, receive help when building life for themselves.
 **People who** work with life , Life works with them.
**People who** show *Gratitude in their Attitude*, Never sink but always float to the top.

# Life Affirmations
The more you do Affirmations the more issues in Life will become clearer to YOU!!!!!

## Allegiance To Life Affirmations

USING THE AFFIRMATIONS EVERYDAY WILL DEVELOP THE COGATIVE- INTERGRATION PROCESS NEEDED TO REGAIN YOUR EMOTIONAL- AWARNESS- POWER FROM THE PLANET CALLED LIFE AWARENESS...

*Affirming to life allows you to:*
*Reclaim your emotions and feel safe!*
*Reclaim your ability to love!*

Start with the first Affirmation, say the affirmation at least once a day. Once you know the first affirmation by heart, you will naturally feel the urge to move to the second affirmation. Do not skip the building process, YOU will not receive benefits quicker, benefits are a result from inner- core growth. Watch how your inner power will start to grow. Practicing the affirmations will start the process of inner- healing needed to allow the development of our innate cognitive awareness prisciousness into an Earth being capable of planetary vision and leadership of our life and purpose to Earth.

# Life Affirmation #1

I am a being or cell of Life with Earth

I value the life force within me.

I respect the life body shared with me.

The love for the Blood of life dwells with in me

The joy for life flows through me

The power of Life surrounds and sustains Me.

The Earth law for life protects Me.
I surrender to life
and ALIVE is how I remain.

# Life Affirmation #2

My allegiance is to Life
I am ready to serve my purpose for living with Life.

I respect the expression of Life as Love for Life with-in me.

The love for life flows thru me

The power for Life sustains and provides for me
The principles that govern Life protect me.
I love our planet Earth and full of its life power is how I remain.

# Power from Life affirmation #3

I am ready to Live for life

I am ready to serve Life
I am willing to serve my birth function and fulfill my purpose as part of the force of life of Earth

The power from life strengthens me.

The essence of Life provides and sustains me.
The principles governing Life guides and protects me.

The power of Earth Life is with me
Fearless is how I remain.

# My allegiance is to my SOUL Purpose

I respect the purpose of Earth emotion within me

I value the life purpose the Nature of Earth has shared with me.
The joy for life power from Earth emotion flows through me
The awareness governing the emotion of Earth guides me.........
The Life force of Earth sustains me.....
The principles governing life in Nature protects me.......
My Life resolve IS to SERVE my life's SOUL PURPOSE towards reaching my destiny for MY Life with Earth .

And fearless, successful in reaching my destiny is how I will remain.

# Life Prosperity #4

My Allegiance is to Life, my Soul, my home with Earth America..

I value the Life shared with me…
I respect the Life purpose given to me..
I love the Life living within me….

The joy for life flows thru me…
I trust the power of Life to thrive, provide and sustain prosperity with me.

The principles of Nature that govern the power of Life protect me against the false perceptions, artificial beliefs, conditions and illusions that create distrust of LIFE and fear of harm and death from man.

I surrender to the force of Life within me, and fearless, confident that life's power will lead me to fulfil my life purpose and reach my destiny. My allegiance is to the power of Life and Alive, fearless, purposeful, and free is how I stand and will remain...

## Health #5

### Building Life Energy-
### Staying Life Enthused   1-3x daily

*My allegiance is to Life, my soul, and my blood of America*

*I value the blood of Life given to me*

*I respect the blood of Life shared with me.*

*I love the life force that flows within me.*

*I trust the power of Life to provide, sustain and thrive with me.*

*Principles that govern Life protect me from the ego, false illusions created by man, and perceptions that bring fear.*

*My allegiance is to stand for life, Earth and America, and focused, fearless, and Life Enthused is how I remain.*

## Affirmation : Gratitude for Life prayer

*"Let Gratitude for having Life, for being a part of Nature of Earth be your Attitude towards Life with Earth."*

I have gratitude for my grace as an part of Life with Earth......
 thank You.....
For creating me to live with-in You.
 Thank you for creating me as a part of your Nature, and
Giving me a function of being with my SOUL.
and a purpose to serve in Life within the SOUL Nature of Earth.......
I respect my home in Earth.
I help keep and build Life of Earth to thrive into the future....

I stand and protect the Nature for Life of Earth. Thank you for Life as a part of our planet SOUL.
Aquechewa ,
Aquecheway

# Collective Allegiance To Life Affirmation

*USING THE COLLECTIVE AFFIRMATION EVERYDAY WILL DEVELOP THE COLLECTIVE COGNITIVE -INTEGRATION PROCESS NEEDED TO REGAIN OUR COLLECTIVE EMOTIONAL AWARENESS FROM THE PLANET EARTH TO OUR LIFE.*

Affirming to our collective blood of Life (TREE) allows us to
Reclaim our Collective emotional security and feel safe with Nature and each other.
Allowing our Collective ability to love, heal and will produce our needs from our soil for our children and each other..

Say these affirmation at least once a day and watch how the connections to our planet Earth with our collective family, start to heal and grow. Unfortunately, we all have experienced violations that has mentally and emotionally conditioned us to live without the emotional experiences we need to develop and grow into an highly functional collective capable of planetary vision and leadership for directing Life as it exists with the planet.

Affirmation as follows:

We who look like the soil of Earth are SOUL workers for the planet Earth……
We exist as a part of the emotion of Life with Earth

The emotion of the Earth as nature- of life produced us
The joy of Life – harmony, is balanced by us

The power of nature – life, is energized by us and will provide for us.
The PRINCIPLES GOVERNING Life – existence, is the power that governs us and will protect us.
Our allegiance is to Our Planet Earth, Our home is with the Earth section America
and awareness of this truth will never be forgotten..

## AMERICA ALLEGIANCE TO ART

We the people created by the Earth,
who look like the SOIL of America
Pledge my Allegiance to our SOIL of
America with the planet Earth
To
Respect the blood of Life within me
And
Value the life from the Nature of America
shared with me
To trust in the fact life within me loves me
Recognizing
The love for life flows through me
The power of America's Nature sustains and
surrounds me
The principles for life of Earth protects me
My Allegiance is to my planet Earth , to the
Covenants for Life with my blood of America
is how
I stand- strong, fearless, alive and free to
serve my life purpose ,is how I will remain.
Ho ho!!!

# The original Emblem of America

AN EMBLEM OF AMERICA.

# Prayers
# Life, Nature & the Earth

**What is prayer?** Prayer is the act used for connecting to our inner life power awareness. Prayer supports and helps direct the force of life.

**The purpose of prayer.**

Prayer is used when we need to connect to our internal essence of awareness to give us life assistance, and directive in our journey to our destiny with Life.

Prayer is how we stay connected to the emotional awareness power living with in us and stay focused on our larger life purpose .

Indigenous Prayers strengthen the person's connection to the life force awareness living with in them.

Recite the prayers and watch your Life grow.

A Prayer for Earth
*By Wisdom Keeper*

# Our *planet* "Earth" Creator of all Life

This Prayer is for you.-To help us save you.

May all that is not of you be removed from You….
May all that is Living in you that has no respect for You ,lose their ability to have will with you
May that which has transformed into you, May you transform it into something that receives no power from You And be returned to dust.
May all that is connected to you but is not a real creation of you, May their existence cease to exist
May that which attempts to destroy you and rule over you, May they be destroyed by the prisciousness of You…
May the people created by you return to their Life purpose for living with You..
May the Power of Life within you Stand Greater than the cancer of death from Man growing inside you.
May the will of Life with you stay stronger than the will of Man that is destroying You…
I send this a prayer to YOU…
My MOTHER OF LIFE - Emotion of Earth
Al-ley lu uh
Hela lu ya..Hal-Lah LU YAAA

## Forgiveness for our Past

I release the pain and suffering from the personal affliction s perpetuated against my emotional and physical being from my parents and stand united with the knowledge my life ultimately came from the blood of Earth in ı forgive my mother and rejoice for the gift of life I have inherited from her.

I take my rightful place in nature, I support the larger purpose for my creation in Life, therefore , I stand with the planetary resolve to keep the life of Earth from death.

### *Earth Meditation*

I affirm I am a Earth being

I am a creation from the blood of the Earth in my Mother

As such I am created as part of the continuation of life and nature of Earth. I belong to my planet Earth

To have a purpose to serve life for Earth.

I am not limited by the physical illusions of mankind. I am created and hold in the essence of my being the spirit of my true mother Earth.

Forgiveness   Prayer

I forgive all the people who didn't have any love for me.

I pray that they may one day heal their wounds to their heart.

I embrace the wounded self of ME, that is hidden from view, you are one with the spirit of Life, and I will always love you just the way YOU ARE.

## Prayer for the Heart

Oh Spirit for life of Earth

May I never get bored of the Life shared with me

May I never stop serving the purpose of Life for me.

May I never get so angry and tired of living that I let go of Life

May I always be full of Life purpose in creating a new future, so I may always feel strong with the love from life in my heart as joy .

# Happiness Prayer

Life grant me the power to help recreate the reality that is one with you living as a part of your organic happiness.

Grant me the trust I need to allow life to blossom in me, and grow into the being of Life, I was created to be.

Give me insight to see beyond the darkness of today, to create a better tomorrow where I can live in life with you creating happiness.

I humbly ask for your guidance, I am ready to follow my heart, building the structures to support life is my service for Life. Joy and Happiness is my reward. And so it will be

HoHo

# Thank you for Loving me

***Thank you*** oh planet Earth for holding on to me as my Life goes through the perils and obstacles created by the allegiance to artificial perceptions created as traps to rob me of my Happiness by the ego of Man.

Thank you for finding me , opening a way for Me.

Thank you for not giving up on me and leading me out of the wilderness of Deception, and Death.

Thank you for opening my eyes so I may embrace and see that it was the Life in me keeping me strong when I could not see the way forward …..

HoHo

## _Morning Prayer_

LIFE – Thank you for sharing another day in your experience with me.

Thank you for giving me another chance to fulfill my function and serve my purpose in the collective journey of the SOUL "LIFE" of Earth.

I give thanks for my health and ask forgiveness for the weakness in perceptions that hinder me from staying focus on keeping LIFE moving forward.

## Indigenous 23rd Psalms

 Life awareness is my Sheppard: I shall not want. it leadeth me to lie down in green pastures: it leadeth me beside the still waters. The force of LIFE restoreth my soul; it leadeth me in the paths of Earth prisciouness. Yea I walk through the valley of death consciousness, I will fear no evil. For the Awareness of Earthlife is with me, its rod and its staff comfort me. Thou prepares a table before me in the presence of mine enemies, thou anointest my life with joy; my cup runneth over with happiness. Surely goodness and mercy shall follow me with happiness all the days of my life with Earth, and I will dwell in my home of Earth forever.

Al·le·lu·jah, ye-ho wah

Al-le-lu- yah, ye-ho wah

Al-le-lu-yah   ye-ho-wah

## Our Creation Prayer

Our Creator, the essence of Nature , our living Earth, who made all Life, be it heaven, soil, sea, the nature of all living being...

Glory be to our planet Earth..

Thy Life is in all, thy purpose will ultimately be done

Grace us this day to stand in face of all challenges against the Life, of our Nature and forgive us for our weakness and failings against the challenges to our nature as a part of our planet Earth Life, as we forgive others for failing their challenges against our nature as a part of our planet Earth life .

Keep us strong against corrupted intellectual temptations and emotional addictions and deliver us from its evil, for thine is the power and the glory for Life everlasting.......

Alleluia, Alleluia, Al-le-lu-ia,........

## Prayer for the Departed
## A Prayer to David

Oh ancestors who live without form. May our voices reach you, and our hearts connect with you. May you watch and walk with us, helping us in guidance as we continue on with our life journey ...

Always knowing that you are with us , we are never alone, your spirit is silently supporting us, cheering us to move forward to reach our destiny. Patiently awaiting for the time when we to will return back to spirit, where we will meet once again.

Alleluia, Alleluia, Al-le-lu-ia,……..Ho HO

# Prayers of Assistance

**Prayer for humility, Prosperity and Earth protection.**
**Light a Green candle**
I come to you for help. My vanity, my pride and my arrogance are keeping me from knowing the love of life and Nature. Grant me the simplicity, which springs directly from Nature and from which greatness comes. Cause me to be fruitful, resisting all temptations to falsify or indulge in exaggerations of my ego. Take from me the corrupt addictions on my instincts, which cause me to wander from my goal, which is to stand with my purpose to nature, Earth and all that is created by its life and to know the power of LIFE is working towards my prosperity in my daily life experience.

**Obtain Courage, Justice, Protection**
**Light a Blue candle**
I trust the principles of life to protect me in time of danger. Grant me the strength to stand strong in the face of injustice which surrounds me. With the force of Life in my heart, I can be calm and courageous, knowing that Principles of life are all encompassing LAW and those who stand in its grace

will surely have no danger, for those who seek it liberation, thou will be set free. Graced this day I pray.

### Help one to be masterful.
### Light a Yellow candle

Mother/ Father of Life release from my heart and mind of the intellectual ego, bitterness, anger, and rebellion. Give me courage and quiet of spirit , and focus of mind. Guide my efforts step by step towards those things which aid all productive efforts in Life, which I can trust, is of truth, value, sensitivity, inquisitiveness, daring, learning, awareness and understanding, and take away all fear of failure or rejection. I trust and allow the force of life within me to lead my endeavors to their highest good.

### To be free from all Evil
### Light a Brown Candle

May the truth of thy Nature light my heart with love and strength and goodness...

Keep me free from the bondage of ignorance and from dependency on any force which stands between me serving my Life purpose so, I may be worthy of receiving life's bountiful grace.

### For Peace and love within family
### Light White candle

I pray for the power of nature to grace the heart of our family with love and connectedness . Help me, I pray, that I may see in others the same feelings I strive to attain in myself... the love for blood of life , family, ancestors that walk with me, the urge for deeper understanding of myself and the knowledge of life, the wisdom to recognize that which I can change ,and that which I cannot.. and the courage to wish them to forgive me my shortcomings ,may I be forgiving of the failings of others. I pray for the strength , the understanding to carry me forward in service to my life purpose , so that I may do my share towards creating a purposeful, loving life for myself and those I love.

### Restoring one's Health

### Light a Red Candle

Take from my heart the attitudes of the past, that gave me fear, bitterness, anger and rebellion against life. Replace these feeling with new hope, joy for life and openness to follow the priscousness of Earth within me,, help me atone and heal the vehicle that houses the power of life within me. Let me testify to thy glory and joy of living and the serenity with which to go forward to a truly happier future...

### Attracting Loving Relationships
### Light a Pink Candle

Mother of Life I come with a need in my heart for knowledge and understanding. I know that all things can work for the good and I ask that this may be revealed to me. We know thy heart desires unity and gives unity for all those who truly desire and is open to those who may live in peace and in Love. Bestow upon us what we truly desire, with the knowledge that life grace will result from the outcome.

### Relief of Sorrow
### Light a White or Brown Candle

At this most difficult time, in my hour of need. Grant me the strength to find solace in the knowledge with deeper understanding and acceptance. The cycle of Life never ends, just transforms into another phase of becoming in the continuation of Life's Journey. Always knowing the spirit of us never dies. Help me take comfort with knowing the ones we hold dear their spirit is with us, living in our hearts, guiding, protecting and helping us move through our life journey to the time when we too will transform into a new phase of becoming in the continuation of my life journey. , where I will meet again united in spirit with all that has sojourned before me……

# Indigenous Meditations

**Changing the course of your Life ship.**

Affirmations help prepare your life ship to change course. Indigenous Meditations are stronger than affirmations and are used when we must change our intellectual attitudes about our perceptions in Life, to allow directional positive change in our flow of Life. Meditation enact the completion of the process.

# First Meditation – Road Opener

 I affirm that my true self is only a cell in the cosmic body within the organic life of Earth, it is not contained within the limits of my body, has no beginning, will never end….

The spirit that I am exist within me underlying my intellectual ego that is my limited sense of personal self..

Earth awareness is God within me , It is of such dimensions that I constantly must strive to understand and embrace it… it is not my body, it is not my name, it is not the perception of identity by which the intellectual world knows me….

Life of Earth awareness simply exist, unchanged by the ever-changing scenes of intellectual living, unaltered by any colorings my personal perspectives may give it. This is my true essence of self and I long to know and become one with it…

I still the questions and imagine hurts, the vain goals of the illusions from my ego. I go deep inside myself to where a deep pool of my life essence rests in absolute tranquility…

In there a center as still as a pinpoint, I find infinity. I look inward, and see Life . All is contained in side the awareness of Life. Here I see I am a cell in the essence of the living Earth I center myself in the essence of my connected awareness, I become detached from my personal attachment to the ideals of my ego...

From this vantage point, I can look upon all differences with equality. I can observe my ego as a person apart, with understanding but with control,,,,,,,,,

I see that I never was what I thought I was, nor was I ever different than what I have always been. The essence of my life is the force with Life of Earth. I declare my unity with Life of Earth. I exercise no will in the things and events of my life, but concentrate always on attunement with the purpose of Life of Earth for me., insofar as I succeed in this I cannot fail, for the awareness of Life's love for me and purposes I serve to life within me will surely be realized, I subject my will for intellectual perceptions of the ego , I surrender my worldly perspective conditioning, I attune myself to the power that flows from the Earth throughout its universe in me, so I can become one .

# Second Meditation- Trusting Life

*When one seeks to attain a deep and abiding joy,*

*when at last one can see that the hidden secret of life is:*

Awareness of Earth wills, the spirit for Life acts, Earth awareness lives in thee All living with life has a purpose to serve for Life.

I search for the secret principles of Life in the depths of my being . I retire inward away from the noises and distractions of the physical world. In my being inner depths of tranquility and peace I find in the core of my being absolute calm.

There I find no desire, no motion, nothing to be hoped for, nothing to lose. All roads and all paths meet and unite here.. I am connected to the center of the essence of Life. Time and space are contracted to a moment on a pinpoint. The planets, stars in the Earths universe are connected to me. I am one with all nature.. The essence which lives in Nature is that which lives in me.

Only one thing is at work throughout creation, only one essence lives in all Earth creations. This is the Life with Earth. I surrender my control from my personality over the will of Life and become the vehicle for the essence within me to direct the use of the life force shared with me. I recognize the power sleeping within me quietly awaiting to activate the resolve of the essence of life within me.. I surrender my need to control, divorce any notions of my life as an individual isolated self. I open the doors without fear to the flow of power of life to work through me..

I sense the essence of life awareness filling my being , molding,, sustaining, lifting, healing the wounds of the past, making me emotionally stronger to follow prisciousness as I become an instrument for the force of life for Earth.

No longer do I need to impose my will over life. I step back and let go to follow the will of life awareness for direction. My intellect becomes its intellect, my body becomes its body, I walk life's journey without fear.

By becoming one with the will of life of Earth I attain the power to prevail over all challenges to our Earth, and its creations…. Each day of my life, I seek to support the development of my emotions, and discipline myself to remove the addictions from the world used to enslave me to the artificial vices of the ego.. I seek no reward, profit, or glory. Yet I receive all rewards for life, knowing that the purpose I serve is as small as a pinpoint yet as large to the universe as life itself. I humbly serve my purpose to the life will of Earth………….

# Third Meditation- Transformation

 All about me I see the infinite, eternal movement of Life of Earth. In the surge of the sea, the flux of the tides, the precise patterns of the heavens.

I see the presence of our creator. The universal organic force of Life of our planet Earth.

It knows where it is going, all things past and present, and future are apparent to life. Our life awareness and its wisdom sees all things to be done and perfect method of doing it.

Therefore I turn over my actions in life reality to the Life awareness within me. No longer will I be guided in my daily tasks by willful promptings of my EGO- intellectual programed indoctrination, but instead I tune inwards to the center of my being, and listen for the inner directive of life awareness that dwells within me to show and guide me to fill my life tasks..

The awareness of Life with Earth is the master and the director of my work, it is all that is and I am being of its being, power of its power, Action of its prisciousness.

No more shall I hunger after the fruits of my labor. They support physical life and I renounce all motives only for personal gain from them. I know that life awareness never blunders, never indifferent, and when it appears that I have failed in some immediate aim. I know it is only to prepare myself for a larger universal accomplishment and to receive longer lasting joy.

I open my mind without fear to following the emotional flow as Life with Earth that governs my Life. I declare there is no obstacle too big or limitation, no lack, no malfunction in my life. The force with life of Earth is governing all my affairs, prevailing every cell in my body.

I align my allegiance with that which is true reality with life of Earth. I throw of the limitations from the crimes committed against my life destiny by artificial forces. In the depts. Of my being, I am no longer a name, a color, a past, a place, I align myself with the pure force of the organic living Earth, that is infinite and eternal, all encompassing.

I am becoming more than a physical expression of Earth creation. That which I truly am. I can never cease to be. I cast aside the false perceptions to be artificial for the world of the ego, , instead accept my truth, my beauty, my purpose for living and become one with the organic planet Earth. The universal force that governs the life awareness of Earth, lives in the truth of my creation , and as long as I serve life, the love from life of Earth will be with me always.....

# Being on Point

*The ego is only an illusion of the intellect. It is artificial. Through whose prison life has no joy; Keeping one from recognizing their truth*

*That Life itself is the power and is the most precious gift....*

Becoming one with the will of Life of Earth, to the eyes of the uninformed it appears the attitude " those who take events in life by the horns and take what they want from Life, get what they want, while those who wait around for someone to give it to them, usually get nothing. "If one takes time to look at the outcomes from aggressively attacking life, they find LIFE itself IS very resilient and formidable enemy, and whatever gains made against the principles governing life is only temporary." The mistake one makes are to identify attunement with aggression. An energized male or female performing in accord with her/his natural function for life operating thru the prisciousness of Earth , naturally gives the appearance of dominant and at times aggressiveness. They appear to mold the events around their lives, because they are an inter-active part of the life events, and since they follow the will for Life awareness of Earth prisciousness, their success often is attributed to their ego will over the life force energy when in truth it was the will of life awareness working thru them.

Recognizing when the will of Life is behind how events happen is the first step in having a stress free joyful experience with life.

# Fourth Meditation- Being on Point

I acknowledge the existence of life prisciousness and I dedicate my life to fulfilling my purpose for life on Earth.

I focus my mind on living in life awareness, each waking moment, seeking to learn more about the life force with in me , seeking to allow its will to direct me forward, longing to experience its essence. In the life of Earth I have my existence.

I see the cognitive force of Life of Earth in every flower, bush, tree, heaven and sea, the warmth of life for Earth's presence as Nature is everywhere.

I consecrate my will to the purpose of life for Earth.

Into whatever dangers I may go, by whatever roads for life I may travel, I know the awareness of life is with me, surrounding me. The essence force with life is my comforter and guide. I am its eyes and its ears. I surrender my self-centered illusions, wants and desires to life.

No longer will I struggle with the events and forces of the Ego of man world, I recognize them, I see them as the ego's will revealing the weakness within me that need to be eradicated and corrected.

I join forces with life awareness of Earth. I attain ascendancy over the thoughts, of my personal ego, I see that I have many goals, can serve many purposes. Though all the confusion and struggle of Ego against the power of life will, the prisciousness of life works serenely towards its purpose, nothing is lost, for in reality there is nothing but the essence of life for Earth.

I surrender my personal longings, vanity, and will to the planetary resolve for my Life.

I enter into a state of pure serenity, peace and joy for living Life

Love for life grows in me as the ruling passion in my life. I know all life created by Earth we are one. They are me, I am they. We are fused, bound and united by the force of nature for life of our planet Earth.....

# Fifth Meditation- Peace of Mind

*Oneness with Earth awareness by following Principles for nature in life dispossesses fear.. A person who lives thru their ego, places their standards and discriminations from self-centered attitudes upon what they accomplishes by exploitation of others, how much material riches he accumulates as a result of exploitation, how much applause is accorded them from the influence on other with his riches, yet it is all in vain, the more their ego acquires the more insecure they become, the more contempt for life they have, as their insecurity grows, the isolation from disconnection to the nature of Earth 'or God keeps them living in a internalized state of FEAR. They Look around and do not know where to cast anchor.*

NO matter the chaos in the outer world created by man, there is within me a place of utter quiet and absolute repose. Here, in the center of my eternal being, my life force meets and unites with the universe of Earth .

Here, I know my true self an Earth being, that is infinite and eternal and is untouched by the artificial world of man.

In time of trouble and trial, I turn within, and my heart mind and energies are restored. In the quietness of my room, in my study, during a solitary walk I let my physical awareness drift to a place of pure life awareness, where the eternal essence for the life force of Earth dwells in all Earth created beings. No time or space is there, no separateness, no isolation,. All is unity, infinite, absolute, and eternal, their lives perfect balance, love, perfect wisdom, perfect serenity, and perfect peace. There is no struggle, no pain, no sorrow, these cannot exist where separateness and time are not...

I see my kinship , with all life created by the nature of Earth, with my people of the soil, of our planet Earth.

Envy, contempt, jealousy, and hate are but corrupted illusions to support the ego, which I banish from my mind. I live in the force of Earth life. I am equal to all life, for I am neither better nor worse than any other life expression created with the nature of Earth.

I banish intolerance, for how can I be intolerant of that which is made by the blood of Earth and in which all life dwells. I view all Earth blooded beings with respect and love, for in them I see another piece of Life with Earth.

I motivate my life with purposefulness, with selflessness, humility and resolve, I banish fear, and peace of mind is mine....

# Sixth Meditation-Health and Well Being

The road to attunement and joy. I seek laughter I accept my body as a creation of Earth.. Earth ordained it., life moves it and nature sustains it.

I know this life force to be greater than myself, to be all encompassing presence that inhabits all life that pervades the Earth universe. The beat of my heart, the function of my tissues, love in response to the perfect order, harmony, and absolute power governing life on Earth.

I need not command the organs of my body to function, perfect function is mine by the simple surrender of my personal will to the force of Life will. Health is mine...

Yet I realize the power of decision is mine that I may take a stand, choose a way, and the cognitive awareness of life will lead me on a path to my highest good. I therefore assert that I release hidden pain in my past memories. I bring to light all memories of violation that prompt in my being feelings of hate, bitterness, rejection,, anger and fear towards living life.

By aligning myself with the force of life, by identifying my being with the cognitive awareness of life principle and purpose., I depose all negative emotions and enshrine insight and reason in their stead. Principle and reason lead me down life's most hazardous path, with perfect composure and absolute surety. I cast negative emotions out of my life forever.

My body functions in harmony with all of Nature, there is perfect integration, assimilation, perfect circulation, and perfect elimination, for there is absolute utility of my body function for Earth.

I follow the path of life prisciousness, for in laughter all chains of anguish disappear.

I take refuge in knowing the essence of Earth's life-force is all knowing power governing Earth and my allegiance to "Life" leads me to inner peace, perfect attunement, strength, health, and vigor.

# Seventh Meditation- Love and Unity

I affirm my love for life, and in that love, I perceive the truth of life eternal love for me. I affirm the presence of Earths eternal force with in me , and in the knowledge of that presence, I sense myself secure forever, enfolded in everlasting arms. The nature of Love is the nature life of Earth.

Accordingly, my knowledge of Life with Earth depends on my love for Life; and in so much as this love possesses me, I possess it and I am illumined. Therefore I consecrate my Life, every fiber of my being to serving the essence of Life with Earth, I give all, ask back nothing. Yet what I give from my small self, that which is incomplete and finite and microscopic, will in the end be returned to me hundredfold from which is whole and complete and infinite.

All about me I perceive the creative forms of Life, and I perceive the force of Earth dwelling in each. There are no different selves in the Universe of Earth, but one self only, one sense of being, one awareness, one I which is eternally and always the absolute Life of Earth. When I love another it is the nature of life I love. When I perceive in each form the Earth Life awareness that inhabits all forms, then I know the presence of Life, and in that knowledge I love Life and not death, my life is whole. I no longer anguish against loneliness, for Life is within me.

No path to solitary, no way too deserted that I may not take it with joy and knowledge of the companionship and comfort of Life awareness. Life awareness guides and prisciousness protects my every step, it leads me in all ways. It's love working through me draws my mates to me cements our relationships, crowns our union with joy, its love working through me attracts friends, makes of my life a testimony to its warmth and everlasting compassion.

# Eighth Meditation- Success for a Purposeful Life

There is a power within me which I can use to overcome all obstacles, solve all problems, a power that flows from the farthest reaches of the Universe of Earth, out of the infinite, omnipotent cognitive awareness prisciousness of Life.

I give over my work, its progress and path to it. Only Life awareness knows the real purpose and actual nature of the things I do and the goals I aspire to, and can chart a perfect course to the destine shore.

No longer do I allow my little self to direct my life and work, for in such egoistic blindness there is only suffering. It is knowledge I seek and joy, and I find them through serving the purpose for my Life.

No matter the negations I encounter, I see beyond them, perceive their other face. All revealing a purpose, each a step in life development, each may be overcome by an inner insight that springs abundance out of lack, expansion out of limitation, success out of failure, victory out of defeat. I know that the priscious governing Life is all things at all times; therefore I affirm the positive.

I call forth atonement from evil, not because I will it, but because I perceive it, because I know that Life reveals to the individual mind that which its awareness is able to perceive.

My cognitive awareness surpasses the limitations of the ego, and soars out to encompass all Earth Life. I affirm my knowledge of Earth life encompassing expression of unity with life in my life, and I accept the challenges to my life as good for my cognitive awareness development. Success is mine, victory, progress, abundance, and joy………

# Ninth Meditation - Creativity

I search the inner depts., of my intellect for that haven of refuge where the essence of life and I meet and are connected as one.

The noises and desires of the demanding outer world fade away, and I retreat ever deeper, through levels of being and awareness to a place of utter repose, of absolute joy, of complete unity, where the barriers are removed between myself and Life awareness.

I lose myself in its essence, and in that releasing I find my greater purpose of self; Life awareness takes my being and makes it an instrument for Life of Earth purpose and creative expression.

Through my mind and body the restless energies of emotion, ever unfolding, dynamically illustrating the unlimited creative sides of its nature.

Whatever impinges itself upon my awareness has a delicate and mystic meaning, and I am aware that nothing is fully developed, finally complete, but that each thing, event, idea is but a partial revelation of a unperceivable larger, magnificent truth. To the emergence of this truth I dedicate myself, for I know that concealed in the heart of every Earth creation in reality dwells the emotion of Life essence. In allowing its expression I discover and move beyond the limitations of the smaller self.

To be is to be a part of the expression of Life spirit of emotion; to grow into the full expression of my life purpose. To that growth, to that becoming of my life. I know that my true self is a part of the essence of Life with Earth, the oneself that pervades the universe of Earth, which inhabits all life, looks out the eyes of every being.

Though allowing my life awareness to work through my life. I truly become creative and unbounded by the limitations of the artificial world of man. I truly become a creative expression of Earth, a instrument of the ultimate artistic expression. I know that all life emotion seeks expression of its essence through beauty, knowledge, and love as the expression of the joy living thru Life of Earth.

# Tenth Meditation - Secret for staying young

Youth is growth, and growth is the measurement of receptiveness to learning. I therefore open my mind to the power in my heart for the love of life, which pervade s the universe of Earth.

I open my heart to Life's love for me, it sustains my being, it uses me for its ends, in the life purpose for Earth I center my mind, through it I attune to my life purpose.

There is a place of pure essence at the center of my being that is timeless, space less and ageless. I anchor myself there, I release all attachment to man-made expectations, limitations, and artificial creations of the ego mind and body, for these are but instruments of the illusions of Man.

My essence of life awareness is not altered by entering a particular body, is not changed by the perceptions of the ego, but remain s always one and constant, above suffering and pain, effort and strife, infinite serenity and omnipotence are my essence and are the qualities I strive to represent my Self. It is the love for life in me that saves me from the deterioration of my life vehicle in flesh, which preserves my life from death.

It is following the Life awareness within me that is strong, wise, and omnipotent. I sustain the channels between my mind and life awareness, remove the separation of the ego, and heal it through attunement. My life reflects the luster from life awareness and joy accompanies me on every new quest, for I know I will find insight, growth leading to new wisdom. Whatever strain, struggle, pain and hardship I experience is temporal, knowing my existence is part of eternity, the force in me keeps me young forever...

# Eveleth Meditation - Tapping into Wealth

Behind the physical world of the senses are more planes of awareness where the true causes of things exist. I affirm that these expended levels are with in me, that my destiny is to know how to work with them, they reveal themselves to me insofar as I direct my being , my will to my purpose for life with Earth.

I know that truth of conditions is not completely revealed by my mental senses, that there is hidden significance in all things. I know this awareness proceeds out of the Nature for life of Earth, and that in its pure form it is essence only, awareness only, similar to my own.

Therefore I affirm my oneness with all of the Nature of Earth. In Nature I perceive the indwelling presence of Life for Earth. It resides in the tree, the flower, the sea, the bird, the animal and ME. It is the observer that sits in the center of each Earth creation. I am not I in a true and real sense, but my life spirit is the awareness of Life. Where I fail to expand my intellect to meet with the constantly expanding awareness of Life is when I limit myself to the form and circumstances of physical life.

Therefore I take refuge in the body and being of life with Earth.. I stand apart from my small minded strivings, concerns and desires, but watch them. They are not me, they are the mental conditions/afflictions from the mental conditioning influenced upon me, as though I exist in the midst of all and participate in all, still I am untouched, and by that very detachment there is unloosed through my Nature the power and the purpose of my Life with Earth.

The resolve for Life of Earth lives through me, the power of Earth and its purpose for my life with Earth is where I stand.

# Twelfth Meditation- Mastery with Life

I resign the dominion of the ego and surrender my life to the inner- life essence of Earth with in me I renounce the priority of sensual stimuli and find within me my own power from nature to originate thought, feelings, action and production. No longer do I exist as reflex to events around me, but now I take up the larger purpose for my existence that descends from higher planes of my mind and sprit. I ally myself with first cause, first purpose, I identify myself as a part of Life with Earth.

I make my life a living testimony for life resolve, surrendering each of my thoughts, feelings, and actions without desire for their fruits. No longer am I enamored in the vain desires of the ego. Fame and money and applause are not ends in themselves, and when sought as such, are traps from which pain and suffering eventually ensue.

I go within myself to a core of my being that is pure essence. There I take refuge turning away from all the superficial demands of the beckoning ego world, yielding my focus to the Earth awareness of life in my blood. Yet I do

 not lose senses of my personal self. Now, I take on a greater awareness, an eternal significance, I expand outward from the center of my essence, beyond all horizons, artificial limitations, seeking to include that which always included me, so that I may know life not only as biophysical nature, but also inclusive with life prisciousness. Thus I lead a mystic resolution of myself with Life of Earth and it and I are one. I am forthwith able to follow the purpose for life upon Earth. I seek not to change that which is nature, but only to understand, to possess identical resolve to act accordance with EarthLife purpose, equal souled to all results, existing always above the conflict, secure in the knowledge of union with the Life resolve of Earth.

## Conclusion

Most readers of this book are interested in using the power of the prayers to help them connect to the power of life within them to attain some objective they seek.

Many do not know exactly what they are looking for from Life, they do know something is missing. The author knows that all indigenous people of the Earth regardless if we are young or old, rich or poor, educated, reclusive or gregarious in manner, or how the circumstances of each life differ from one another. We all seek union with our Source, our common quest to unite and become functional doing our ultimate task and purpose for our lives.

Life cognitive awareness is absolutely necessary to enable us to be what we ought to be- to pursue our natural good in our natural way. Yet many find themselves trapped in societal bonds not of our own making and in our efforts to break free, we build prisons of our own. . Some of these traps that in prison us are, Pride, elitism,, vanity, selfishness, narcissism, dishonesty, fear, and prejudice against ourselves. These attributes must be removed from our thoughts, and must be replaced with those qualities of thoughts which permit us the ultimate in human life awareness and growth, that leads us towards vibrant , productive, healthy and joyful experiences with life..

Start now, to heal from emotional wounds, and regain your natural emotional abilities for growth, and experience the joy of Living. Retreats are offered to all indigenous people of the soil, in West Virginia Mountains, North America in the Summer and in the winter they are offered in Belize, Central America .

For more info go to www.fiaah.org Institute for Indigenous America Studies @ www.indigenousamericastudies.institute
Please take advantage of them while they last.
It will be up to you to free yourself from the shackles of small mindedness. you do have the power to become one with your life, so you can flourish again. Reclaim your Life today,
***The Indigenous Peoples of the Earth Book of Prayer*** will help you get there.
Share the joy, to order Prayer books, send email to admin@fiaah.org

# "Embrace Life"
# One day at a time!!!!!!!

www.ingramcontent.com/pod-product-compliance
Lightning Source LLC
Chambersburg PA
CBHW072100290426
44110CB00014B/1767